The EMDR Flip Chart
Copyright © 2024 Megan Salar

Published by
PESI Publishing, Inc.
3839 White Ave
Eau Claire, WI 54703

Cover and interior design by Emily Dyer
Editing by Jenessa Jackson, PhD

ISBN 9781683737964 (print)
ISBN 9781683737988 (ePDF)
ISBN 9781683737971 (KPF)

All rights reserved.
Printed in the United States of America.

Welcome to *The EMDR Flip Chart*

Trauma and complex trauma can be overwhelming and debilitating. When working with clients with these conditions, it can sometimes be difficult to even know where to begin. One revolutionary treatment modality that has shown it *is* possible to heal from trauma and other mental health challenges is eye movement desensitization and reprocessing (EMDR). This powerful therapeutic tool has the ability to help clients break free from the wounds of their past, transform their lives, and identify the value within themselves.

This flip chart is designed to help you delicately and effectively deliver EMDR with your clients. In particular, its primary focus is to assist you in developing strong EMDR resources that you can incorporate throughout the treatment process, as well as to provide you with visual tools for navigating through EMDR targets, protocol setup, and more. It is intended only for qualified EMDR-trained therapists who have gone through basic training. On each page of the flip chart, you'll find a client-facing page (in color) with a dry-erase surface that allows for customization and reuse, as well as a corresponding therapist-facing page (in grayscale) that contains sample scripts you can use to guide clients through the protocol.

By using the tools in this flip chart, you can provide your clients with an anchor along their EMDR journey, helping them feel more secure in knowing what to expect and providing them with clear steps to address target issues along their path to healing.

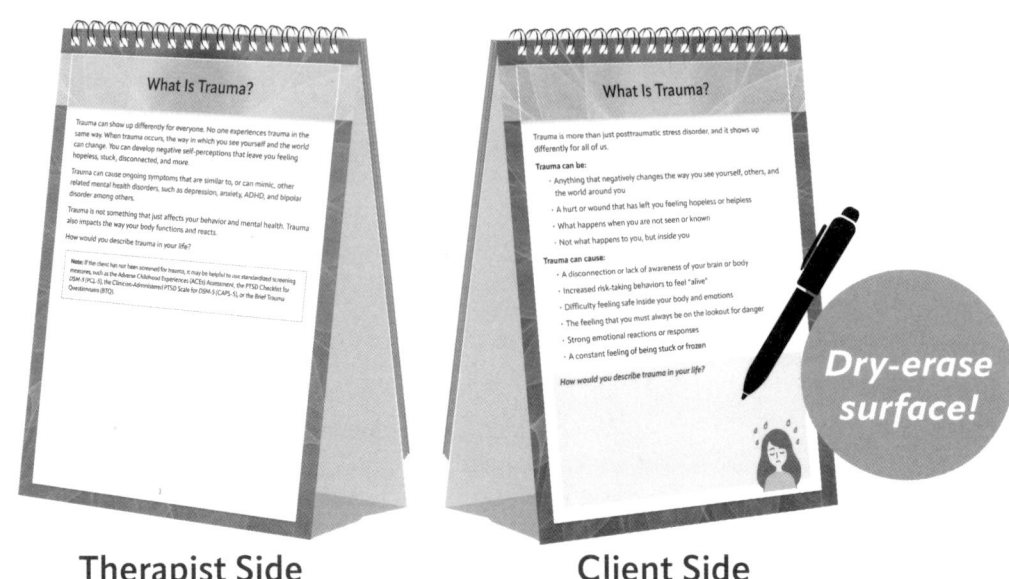

Therapist Side   Client Side

Table of Contents

What Is EMDR? 1

The EMDR Process 2

What Is Trauma? 3

How Trauma Can Manifest 4

How the Brain Responds to Triggers and Threats of Danger 5

How the Body Responds When It Is Stressed and Triggered 6

Trauma Memories Versus Normal Memories 7

How the Brain Can Heal Itself 8

Timeline of Events and Resiliency Factors 9

Bilateral Stimulation 10

Container Exercise 11

Your Restoration Team 12

Calm, Peaceful Place 13

Anchoring Exercise 14

Your EMDR Journey 15

Negative and Positive Cognitions 16

Emotions, Body Sensations, and Intensity 17

Desensitization Part 1 18

Desensitization Part 2 19

Working Through Blocks 20

What Is EMDR?

When you get an injury, your body has a natural healing process. For instance, if you get a small cut or scratch, it will typically heal on its own over time.

Depending on the size or significance of the injury, you may need additional support in helping your body be able to fully recover, such as medicine, stitches, or some other treatment.

Your brain goes through a similar process of healing and recovery when it is injured—even from emotional wounds. And just like your body, sometimes your brain needs support to fully mend.

EMDR is a treatment option that can help your healing continue. It is one of the leading evidence-based and researched treatment modalities for treating a variety of mental health disorders.

What Is EMDR?

EMDR, which stands for eye movement desensitization and reprocessing, is a treatment option that can help your brain fully heal from difficult things you have experienced.

EMDR helps you:

- Get "unstuck" from intense feelings and emotions
- Alleviate the pain associated with past traumatic experiences
- Aid your brain in fully and naturally healing
- Create new meaning of negative past experiences
- Improve your sense of self-worth

The EMDR Process

EMDR is made up of eight phases, which you can also think of as steps:

1. **History taking and treatment planning:** To begin, we will gather information about your history, trauma, and current symptoms. We'll then develop a treatment plan and goals.

2. **Preparation:** During this phase, we will continue working to establish trust, and you will be educated on the EMDR process. You will learn about bilateral stimulation and begin incorporating it with resourcing and coping techniques.

3. **Assessment:** Here, we'll pick a specific target to focus on. This can be a memory, experience, or image that is causing you distress. We will also identify any beliefs, emotions, and sensations related to this target.

4. **Desensitization:** At this point, we will begin using bilateral stimulation (through eye movements, tapping, audio, or other methods) as we focus on the selected target. This phase aims to reduce the emotional charge of the target identified in phase 3.

5. **Installation:** Once the emotional charge is reduced, you will focus on installing, or strengthening, the positive belief that you identified during phase 3. This will help to replace your negative beliefs related to the traumatic memory.

6. **Body scan:** Here, you will check for any physical tension or sensations related to the trauma that may still be present, or you may simply notice the physical relief that you are experiencing.

7. **Closure:** At the end of each reprocessing session, we'll discuss all the progress you've made during that session. We can revisit any resourcing or relaxation techniques, if needed, to assist you in feeling grounded and safe.

8. **Re-evaluation:** At the next session, we'll discuss and assess your progress since the last session and address any remaining issues that you would like to focus on next.

Phases 1 and 2 can take several sessions to complete. Phases 3 through 7 are done in one session, and these phases will be repeated until you feel that you have addressed all the targets that you want to heal and work through.

Each of these phases includes a lot of steps within, but rest assured that I will guide you through these steps in a more simplistic way as we go.

The EMDR Process

Step 1  You will explore parts of your history and identify your hopes and goals, all while we continue building trust and safety.

Step 2  You will learn about why you respond the way you do and how EMDR can be useful for these reactions. Here, you will start to learn about bilateral stimulation while developing basic coping and resourcing skills to help you manage your feelings and emotions. This is one of the most important steps of EMDR.

Step 3  You will identify something you want to focus on. This could be a current struggle, a past event, or something in the future that feels daunting. You will work with me to identify a specific issue and the related symptoms you are experiencing.

Step 4  We will then explore this issue further by adding bilateral stimulation until things improve (and don't worry, they do!).

Step 5  We will work to install a new positive belief about yourself related to this trauma that you are working on.

Step 6  We will check in with your body and how you are feeling, identifying any changes that you are experiencing.

Step 7  At the end of each session or at your next follow-up session, we will discuss what you learned about your experience, and I will share my insights with you.

Step 8  You will identify another area of focus that you would like to work on improving, and then we will repeat steps 3 and 4 until you have finished resolving any of these trouble areas.

Typically, this process can last 3 to 12 months or until you feel that you have addressed everything that you want to resolve.

What Is Trauma?

Trauma can show up differently for everyone. No one experiences trauma in the same way. When trauma occurs, the way in which you see yourself and the world can change. You can develop negative self-perceptions that leave you feeling hopeless, stuck, disconnected, and more.

Trauma can cause ongoing symptoms that are similar to, or can mimic, other related mental health disorders, such as depression, anxiety, ADHD, and bipolar disorder, among others.

Trauma is not something that just affects your behavior and mental health. Trauma also impacts the way your body functions and reacts.

How would you describe trauma in your life?

> **Note:** If the client has not been screened for trauma, it may be helpful to use standardized screening measures, such as the Adverse Childhood Experiences (ACEs) Assessment, the PTSD Checklist for *DSM-5* (PCL-5), the Clinician-Administered PTSD Scale for *DSM-5* (CAPS-5), or the Brief Trauma Questionnaire (BTQ).

What Is Trauma?

Trauma is more than just posttraumatic stress disorder, and it shows up differently for all of us.

Trauma can be:

- Anything that negatively changes the way you see yourself, others, and the world around you
- A hurt or wound that has left you feeling hopeless or helpless
- What happens when you are not seen or known
- Not what happens to you, but *inside* you

Trauma can cause:

- A disconnection or lack of awareness of your brain or body
- Increased risk-taking behaviors to feel "alive"
- Difficulty feeling safe inside your body and emotions
- The feeling that you must always be on the lookout for danger
- Strong emotional reactions or responses
- A constant feeling of being stuck or frozen

How would you describe trauma in your life?

How Trauma Can Manifest

Trauma can cause a myriad of symptoms and responses. When you experience something that threatens your safety or well-being, your brain and body work hard to protect you from experiencing any type of similar threat in the future. That means when your brain or body senses a reminder of a past threat, you can feel triggered or reactive. This is your brain and body's defense system attempting to safeguard you.

When you are triggered, your body releases stress hormones known as *cortisol* and *adrenaline* into the bloodstream. This causes your heart rate to increase, your breathing to become rapid, and your body to become more stiff and rigid—all of which prepare you to be on guard to ensure your safety and survival.

These higher levels of cortisol and adrenaline may also contribute to some of the physical symptoms you might be experiencing. Know that these symptoms are common and normal when it comes to experiences of trauma that have been left unresolved.

The good news is that these symptoms can improve once we explore your triggers and work to reprocess and desensitize them with EMDR.

How Trauma Can Manifest

Place a check mark next to any of the following symptoms you experience:

- ☐ Tension headaches or muscle aches
- ☐ Bowel problems (e.g., stomachaches, irritable bowel syndrome, constipation)
- ☐ Difficulty concentrating or an inability to focus
- ☐ Heightened startle response to noises or touch
- ☐ Frequent colds or illnesses (weak immune system)
- ☐ Increased addictive or compulsive behaviors (e.g., alcohol, drugs, shopping, eating)
- ☐ Emotional mood swings, depression, anxiety, or bouts of anger
- ☐ Nightmares, flashbacks, vivid dreams, or other sleep disturbances
- ☐ Tendency to isolate yourself or feel detached from others
- ☐ Difficulty trusting others or feelings of betrayal
- ☐ Self-blame, survivor guilt, or shame
- ☐ Diminished interest in everyday activities or things you once enjoyed
- ☐ Paranoia, fear, or difficulty feeling safe
- ☐ Loneliness or disconnection from others
- ☐ Struggles feeling safe or trusting in relationships

How the Brain Responds to Triggers and Threats of Danger

You can think of the brain as having three main areas of functioning. These areas are similar to a stop light:

1. The front part of your brain, just behind your forehead, is your prefrontal cortex and what we will refer to as your **green light region**. This is where your brain is able to function and operate smoothly. This part of your brain helps you feel safe and grounded, helps you balance between logic and emotion, allows you to weigh pros and cons, helps you sift through emotions, and is in charge of problem solving and brainstorming.

2. The middle part of your brain, or the **yellow light region**, includes your amygdala. This part of your brain, known as your emotional brain, assesses if you are in danger and need to react or if you are safe and can relax. Just like a yellow light, it tells you to use caution and be on the lookout for danger.

3. The back part of your brain, or the **red light region**, is very similar to a stop light in that it cues you to stop. This part of your brain, known as the brainstem, is where your survival instincts kick in: fight, flight, fawn, faint, or freeze. It is important to know that there is no logic in this region of your brain. Just like a traffic light goes from yellow to red, this part of your brain can quickly initiate a shutdown or "red light" response should it encounter a threat or a reminder of past experiences of trauma.

Just as a stop light cannot show two colors at the same time, this is also true for your brain. Your yellow light region either determines that you are safe (green light) or in danger (red light). If you are operating from the red light, you will be unable to make well-thought-out, rational decisions.

Our goal during treatment will be to get your green light region back online and help your brain get out of the red.

How the Brain Responds to Triggers and Threats of Danger

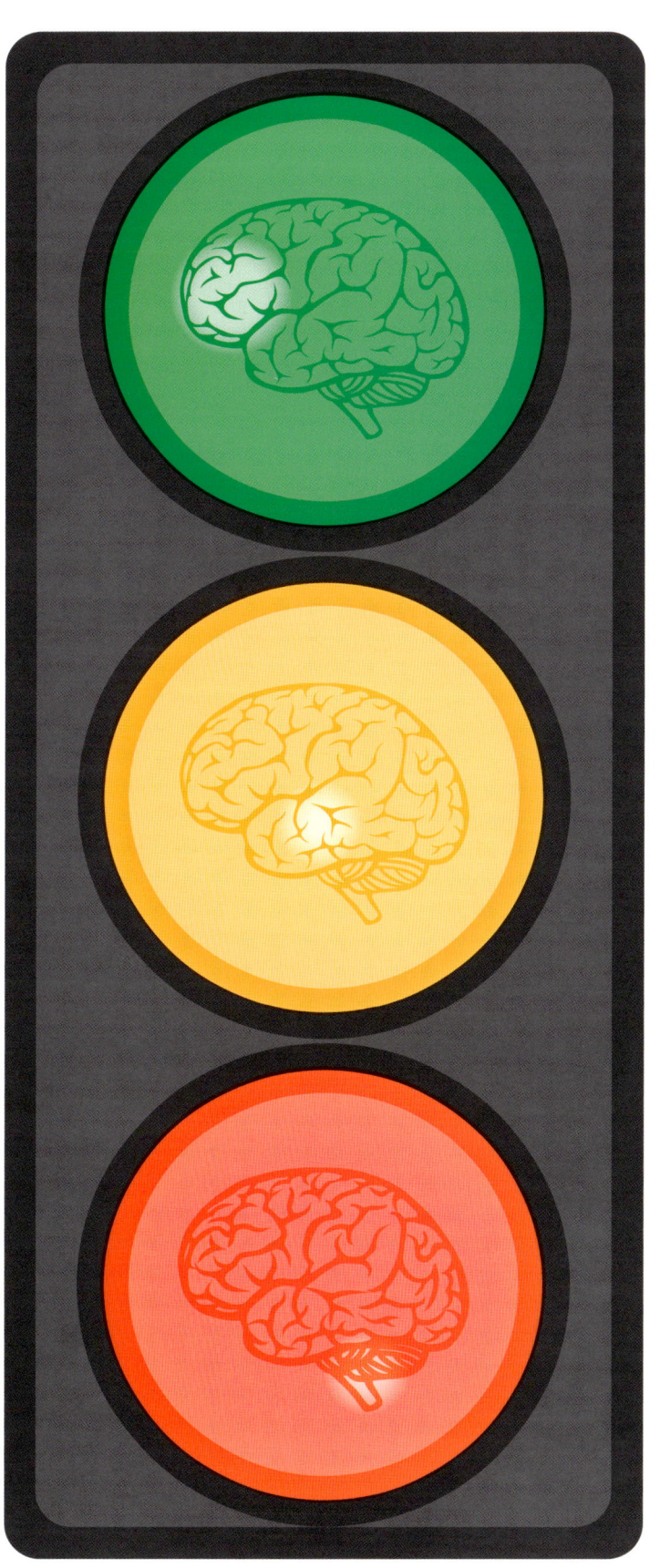

Green Light
The rational part of the brain that balances between emotion and logic

Yellow Light
The emotional part of the brain that is cautionary and assesses for danger or threat

Red Light
The survival part of the brain that activates the fight, flight, fawn, freeze, or faint survival response

How the Body Responds When It Is Stressed and Triggered

We are going to start by identifying some different stressors, or triggers, that you encounter in your day-to-day life and locate where in the body you experience emotions and sensations related to these triggers.

To begin, let's identify a trigger that causes you to feel anxious or stressed.

Then use the body diagram to draw, circle, or label the parts of your body where you experience physical sensations when this trigger occurs. Our goal is to help you identify the different ways your body reacts to triggers and stressors. This will help you start becoming more aware of your physical sensations and reactions.

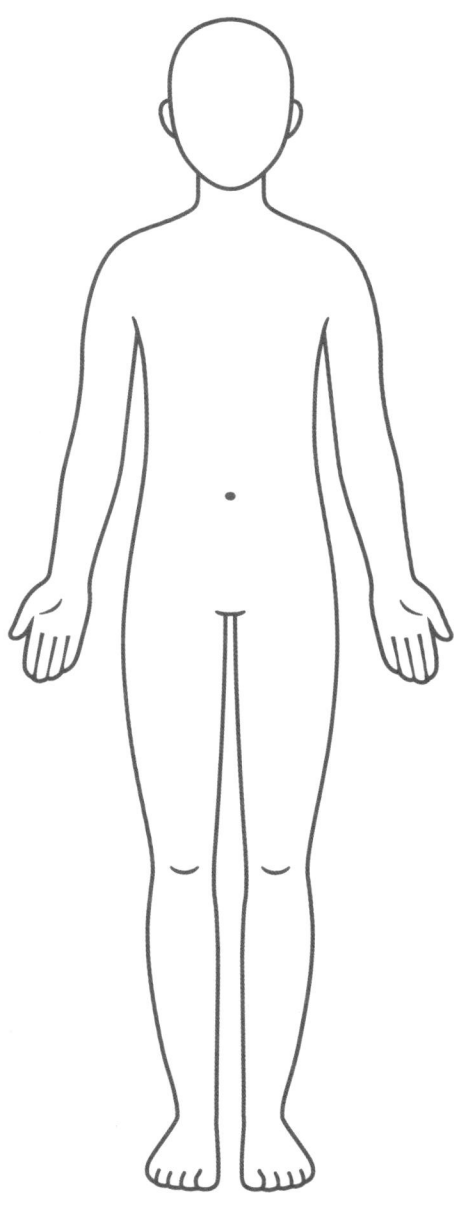

How the Body Responds When It Is Stressed and Triggered

Use the body diagram on this page to identify where you tend to notice responses in your body when you are triggered or activated. Then describe what sensations you notice with these triggers.

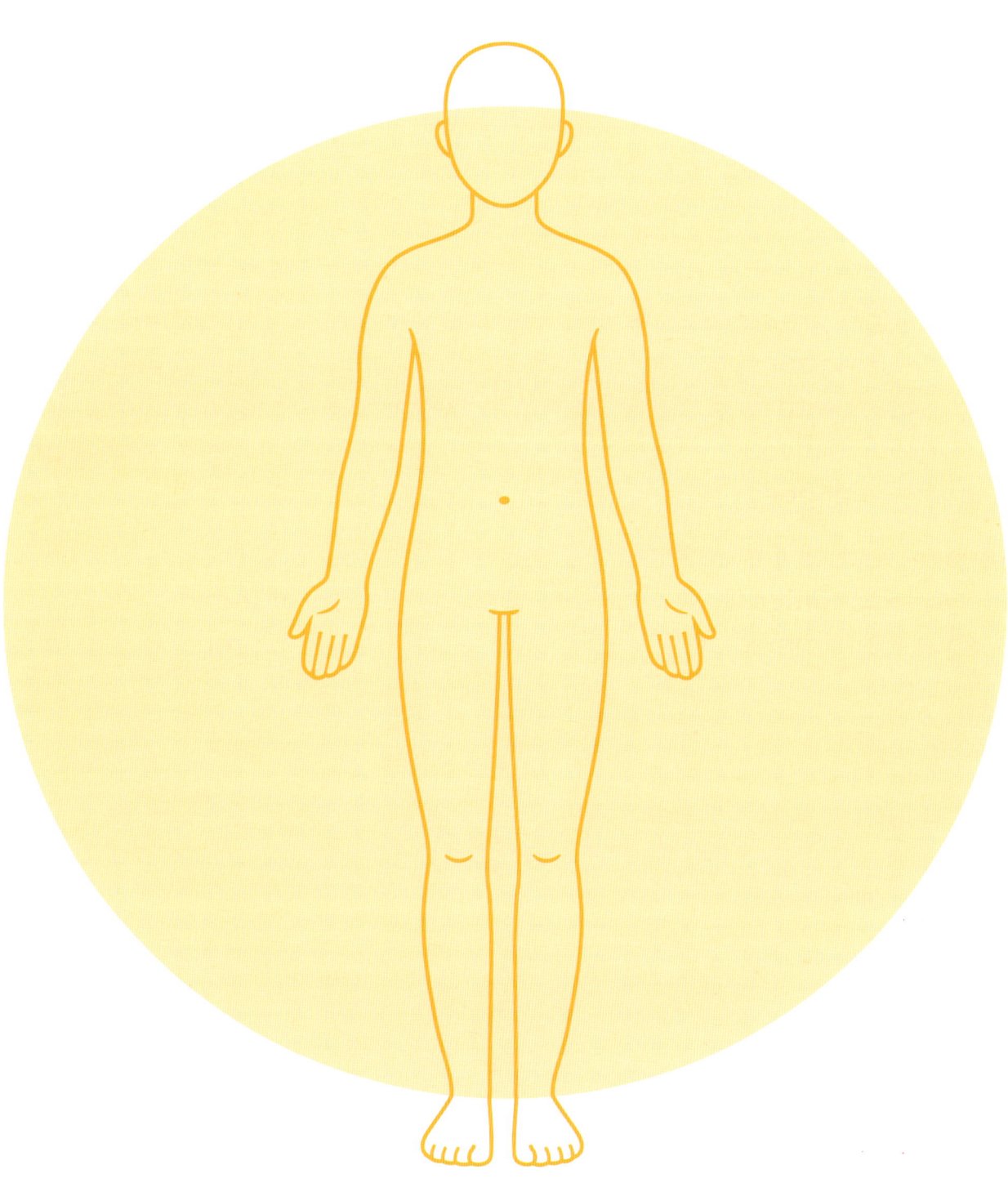

Trauma Memories Versus Normal Memories

Normal memories typically include details of things we have learned, as well as things that are significant and meaningful to us, like holidays, special events, and so on. These memories include a great amount of detail and take on a narrative or story format that encodes the events around and during this time period.

When trauma occurs, your brain becomes less concerned with storing the narrative details of the event and becomes more concerned with storing detailed sensory or emotional information you experienced at the time, including specific feelings, smells, or sounds. As a result, trauma memories are often fragmented and scattered, meaning you can only recall bits and pieces rather than the narrative of what occurred.

Normal memories are stored in your conscious awareness, but trauma memories are stored deep in your subconscious memory. Therefore, trauma memories may be difficult to access with language or verbal expression. You may also find it difficult to put to words what you are feeling since the logical, verbal region of the brain is usually impaired or goes offline in response to trauma.

As trauma memories are stored in their own neural network, they can be activated any time you encounter sensory or emotional reminders of the trauma. When this occurs, your brain immediately feels that it is in danger and prepares you to react.

Trauma Memories Versus Normal Memories

Normal Memories

Non-traumatic memories are stored like a narrative or story with a beginning, middle, and end.

They often have a sequence and order to the way they are encoded in your brain.

Trauma Memories

Trauma memories are stored as emotions, images, and sensations deep in your subconscious.

They are not stored in sequential order like a story.

They are often fragmented and scattered, meaning you can only recall bits and pieces.

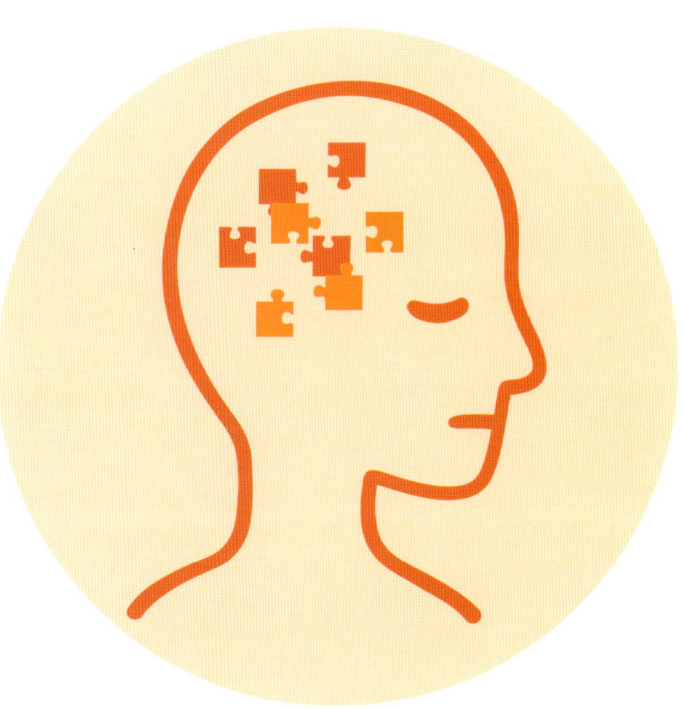

How the Brain Can Heal Itself

When you have experienced traumatic or difficult experiences, they can become stuck in your brain and body, which may make it difficult to move forward or cope with daily stressors. Essentially, your brain's natural healing process, which is known in EMDR as *adaptive information processing* (AIP), has gone offline.

With EMDR, we are going to help your brain resume its natural capacity for healing while working through past negative experiences. This will allow you to decrease the amount of triggers that you face, and you will be much better able to manage your day-to-day life without getting activated. You will feel more in control of your life and feel more positive about yourself.

How the Brain Can Heal Itself

Our brains have a natural healing process, which we refer to within EMDR as the *adaptive information processing* (AIP) *system*.

Through the use of EMDR, we can access the AIP system and help get your traumatic memories unstuck or reorganized in a way that is more meaningful and less disruptive.

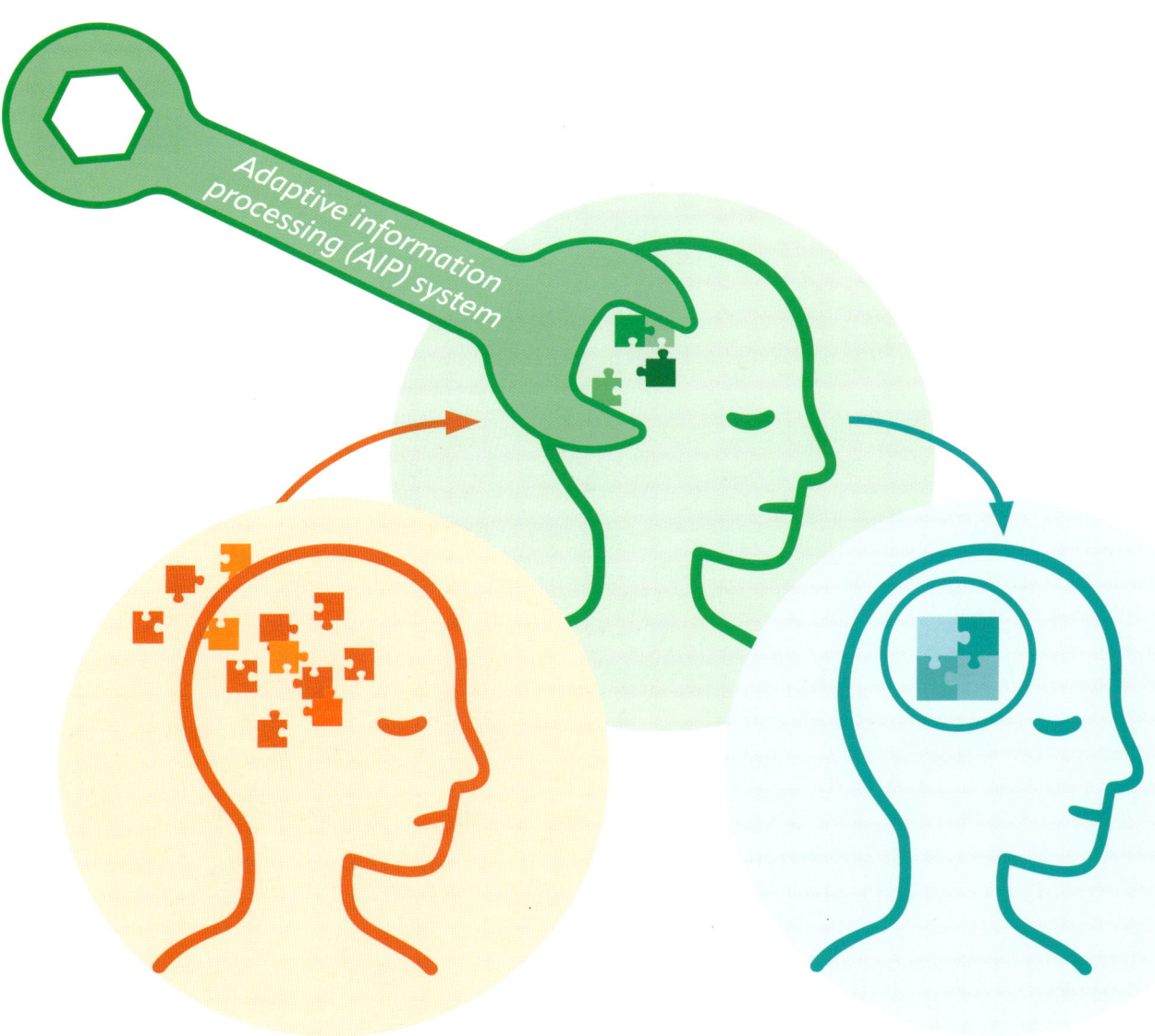

Timeline of Events and Resiliency Factors

Let's begin to explore some of the events in your life that may be causing you symptoms of distress.

We are going to start by creating a timeline of events. We can take our time with this exercise, as this may feel overwhelming, so be gentle with yourself as we walk through this process. We can take as much time as needed. Some people find it helpful to just start with a certain period of time and build upon this in upcoming sessions.

As we construct your timeline, we will also identify your own personal resiliency factors. These are things that helped you to cope during these difficult times in your life.

In the column labeled *Negative Life Experiences*, identify difficult life experiences that you have faced. These can be things that you directly experienced, learned about, were told happened, or witnessed.

In the column labeled *Positive Life Experiences*, identify any of the positive things that you enjoyed, experienced, or leaned on during these years that gave you a sense of hope or helped you endure. These can be accomplishments you are proud of, new skills or hobbies you developed, friends you made, positive or favorite memories, people who encouraged or supported you, or favorite sports, musicians, books, movies, or characters that inspired hope, creativity, or freedom.

Timeline of Events and Resiliency Factors

Negative Life Experiences	Age	Positive Life Experiences
	0	
	5	
	10	
	15	
	20	
	25	
	30	
	35	
	40	
	45	
	50	
	55	
	60	
	65	
	70	
	75+	

Bilateral Stimulation

EMDR uses a unique tool called *bilateral stimulation* or *dual awareness* to help initiate the natural healing process within your brain that you have been learning about. This can involve the use of eye movements, tapping, safe havening, auditory stimuli, or tactile stimuli. These different forms of bilateral stimulation help your brain get out of fight, flight, fawn, faint, or freeze mode and operate in a more balanced way. We'll work together to find the type of bilateral stimulation that works best for you.

The left and right movements associated with bilateral stimulation mimic what occurs during rapid eye movement (REM) sleep. During REM sleep, your brain continues to process events it has experienced during the day. Research has found that when both hemispheres of your brain are engaged during REM sleep, your brain has a greater ability to access, process, and resolve memories in a way that is more adaptable and less disruptive for you over the long term. That means your brain is better able let go of things that were once traumatic and see them in a new way. However, for this to occur, both sides of the brain must be engaged and working together, which is where EMDR and bilateral stimulation will be helpful.

Bilateral Stimulation

EMDR uses a special technique called *bilateral stimulation*, which typically involves the use of touch, sound, or eye movements that occur in a rhythmic motion, from right to left.

This type of stimulation helps both sides of your brain (emotion and logic) come online and work together so you can more readily use reason, logic, and emotion to better make sense of things.

Here are the different types of bilateral stimulation that you can try:

- **Eye movements:** Following a light from right to left

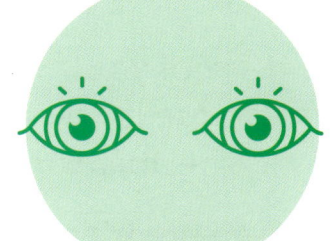

- **Tapping:** Crossing your arms over your chest and tapping your hands from right to left

- **Audio:** Using headphones that alternate sound from right to left

- **Tactile:** Holding vibrating buzzers that vibrate from right to left

Container Exercise

The container exercise is an EMDR exercise that we will use to help you contain any thoughts, feelings, emotions, or memories that are causing disruption for you. Let's begin:

1. Think of an object—either real or imagined—that you can use for this exercise. Your container will want to have some lid or lock that allows you to secure things inside it. Some examples may be a treasure chest, a jar, a suitcase, or a safe.

2. Once you have something in mind, let's add some bilateral stimulation of your choice.

3. As you think of your container, notice its size, its color, and how you would open and close it. Notice if it can keep things soundproof, if it is expandable, or if it has the ability to shrink things down once they are inside.

4. Take a deep breath in and out as we stop the bilateral stimulation. What did you notice?

5. We are now going to place some recent stressors, worries, fears, or unwanted memories or thoughts inside your container. Once you have something in mind, we will start the bilateral stimulation again.

6. Imagine opening up your container and putting whatever you'd like inside. Take as long as you need to do this. If anything feels too difficult to put inside, you may envision someone there to help you.

7. Once you feel everything is inside, go ahead and nod for me. [*Wait for client to nod.*] Now envision closing or sealing your container. As you do this, know that you can return to this exercise anytime you need to add to or take away from the container. We can now stop your bilateral stimulation.

> **Note:** This skill can be used in and out of session when the client experiences distress, unwanted emotions, flashbacks, or other disturbances. Check in with the client on a weekly basis to see what they've put in the container so it does not become forgotten or a method of dissociation.

Container Exercise

Think of a container or object, real or imaginary, that can be used to hold your stress, worry, fear, or unwanted thoughts or memories. The only criterion is that your container should have some lid or lock that allows these things to be contained.

Your Restoration Team

For this exercise, we'll work together to create a support system for you, known as your *restoration team*. Your restoration team can include anything that you find helpful—be as creative as possible! You might include fictional characters from books or movies, musicians, animals, objects, symbols, people in your life (dead or alive), imaginary people that you create in your mind, or anything else that resonates with you. Let's begin:

1. We will start with some bilateral stimulation as I prompt you to think of certain categories of people you can include on your restoration team. These are just suggested categories that may or may not resonate with you.

2. First, think of a someone or something that would represent acceptance or unconditional love to you.

3. Next, think of someone or something that would represent protection or strength.

4. Continue by thinking of someone or something that would represent wisdom or insight.

5. Now, think of someone or something that would represent inspiration.

6. Finally, think of yourself at your best—the person you are striving to become.

7. Take a deep breath in and out as we stop the bilateral stimulation. What did you notice?

8. We are going to have you notice all of these figures, people, or objects once more as we add some bilateral stimulation.

9. Bring all of these figures, people, or objects to mind once more. As you do, just notice what they would want to remind you of. What message would they want to leave you with or encourage you with? Who would they tell you to remember that you are?

10. Take a deep breath in and out as we stop your bilateral stimulation.

Note: Encourage the client to select figures, objects, or resources that have not harmed them or caused any type of trauma or associated trauma. If it is difficult for some clients to think of certain categories, meet them where they are. You can also use qualities that the client already embodies if it is difficult for them to come up with certain categories. These categories can be used or developed at any time and are interchangeable. Encourage the client to use these in and outside of session when they need support.

Your Restoration Team

What or who comes to mind for you when you think of acceptance or unconditional love?

What or who comes to mind for you when you think of protection or strength?

Who or what comes to mind for you when you think of wisdom or insight?

Who or what inspires you?

Can you describe who you want to be?

Calm, Peaceful Place

This exercise will help you to calm yourself when needed. Let's begin:

1. Bring to mind a safe, calm, relaxing, or peaceful place—either real or imagined—that you have been or want to experience. Once you have a place in mind, go ahead and tell me what it is.

2. We will start adding some bilateral stimulation as you take a deep breath in and out, thinking of this place as vividly as you can and noticing as many details as possible. Take a deep breath in and out, and when you're ready, we will stop the bilateral stimulation.

3. Can you share what you had come to mind?

4. We are now going to pick a word or mantra that best represents this place. For example, you might choose something like *calm*, *peaceful*, *relaxed*, or *free*. What comes to mind for you?

5. We will return to adding some bilateral stimulation as you think about this place once more, noticing all its specific details as clearly as you can. As you do so, bring to mind your mantra or word that represents this place.

6. Imagine taking the feeling of this place along with your mantra and allowing it to flow through you, starting at your head and working down throughout your entire body. Once you feel completely relaxed, stop the bilateral stimulation.

7. Now, we will test the strength of this place. Think of a stressor you currently have going on in your life.

8. Taking a deep breath in and out, begin bilateral stimulation and think of this calm place again, noticing all the details as strongly as you can along with your mantra. Continue to allow the thoughts, feeling, and images of this place to flow through you. When you feel settled, take a deep breath in and stop the bilateral stimulation.

> **Note:** If the client struggles to find a place, prompt them to think of somewhere they have always wanted to visit. If they struggle with imagery, use a picture of the place for them to focus on. If they experience intrusive thoughts, invite them to imagine putting a protective wall around their place, to choose a different location, or to return to the container exercise.

Calm, Peaceful Place

Think of a place—either real or imagined—that you have been or would like to go that would represent an overall feeling of calm or peacefulness to you. This could be a place that reminds you of a lot of positive feelings and emotions.

Anchoring Exercise

This is another resourcing skill that can help you manage triggers and stressors. This exercise will require you to think of one of your most cherished or favorite memories or experiences in life. Let's begin:

1. Describe the experience you are thinking of—including your age, what was taking place, all the sensory details, and any specific body sensations, emotions, and thoughts.

2. Now let's strengthen this memory by adding bilateral stimulation as you bring it to mind. You're turning the volume up on this memory or making it brighter and more vivid in your mind. Pull the memory closer to you, noticing all you felt during this time that made it feel special. [*BLS should be very rapid, lasting approximately 20 to 30 seconds.*]

3. Take a deep breath in and out as we stop the bilateral stimulation. Can you share with me what you noticed?

4. Let's enhance the positive sensations of this memory once more. Take another deep breath in and out, starting the bilateral stimulation again as you notice the positive memory. [*BLS should be very rapid, lasting approximately 20 to 30 seconds.*]

5. Stopping the bilateral stimulation and taking a deep breath in and out, choose an anchor word that represents this memory or the feeling you get from this experience. For example, you might choose something like *strong*, *unstoppable*, or *accomplished*. What word is coming up for you?

6. Beginning bilateral stimulation again, think of this memory as vividly as you can. You will now state your anchor word out loud three times. Then we will stop bilateral stimulation.

7. Now let's use this anchor word to help you shift your feelings or thoughts. Bring up something that has been causing you distress.

8. Starting bilateral stimulation, focus on this stressor for a moment. Now, state your anchor word out loud three times again and then stop the bilateral stimulation.

9. What shifted from the distressing memory? Some people find that they are unable to think of the stressor or that it doesn't feel as upsetting anymore. You can use this as a way to shift your focus if you need to outside of session.

Note: If the client did not notice a change in their feeling state, it may help to change the anchor word to something that fits more appropriately.

Anchoring Exercise

What is one of your most cherished or favorite memories or experiences?

What is a word that would represent this memory or experience?

Your EMDR Journey

Now that we have built some resourcing skills, we are going to begin setting up an issue to target with EMDR. We will keep this process brief so that we can move into the next phase of EMDR, where we will work to desensitize and work through this target issue. Let's start by identifying a presenting issue that you would like to focus on:

1. What is the presenting issue or memory that you would like to work on or focus on during this session? [*You do not need a lot of details here, so keep this brief. The rest of the information around this event will present itself when you get into processing.*]

2. What feels like the worst part of this memory to you? What stands out the most to you? This could be a feeling, a thought, a sensation, or something else. [*Again, do not ask for specific details here. You just want to identify the most salient part of the issue.*]

> **Note:** Use the next several pages to set up the protocol before proceeding to desensitization. The protocol should not be used until the client has successfully been able to use the resourcing skills introduced on prior pages.

Your EMDR Journey

We will be using the next several pages to set up your EMDR session.

As we begin, what is the issue you would like to focus on today?

When you think of this issue, what stands out the most or feels the worst about it?

Negative and Positive Cognitions

We are now going to identify the beliefs you hold about yourself as a result of this issue, as well as what you would like to believe about yourself instead:

1. When you bring up this issue and the worst part, what does it lead you to believe about yourself? Use the list of negative cognitions to help you identify a belief that best fits.

2. Instead of this belief, what do you wish you could feel about yourself instead? Or what do you wish you could believe that would make you feel that you can handle this better? Use the list of positive cognitions to help you select a belief that best fits.

3. When you bring up this issue and the worst part, how true does this positive belief feel to you right now on a scale of 1 to 7, with 1 being "completely false" and 7 being "completely true"?

> **Note:** Your goal here is to assist the client in identifying the ways they have internalized the target issue they are focusing on. Ultimately, you are looking for the meaning the client has given this experience. The client can choose any negative cognition from the list provided. It is normal for them to select more than one, but you will want the client to try to choose the one that fits the best or feels the strongest. They should focus on only one positive cognition as well, one that does not yet feel completely true. If the client selects a positive cognition that they rate at a 6 or 7 on the Validity of Cognition (VOC) scale, you will want to encourage them to select a different positive cognition that they would like to work to believe more.

Negative and Positive Cognitions

As you consider the issue we are targeting for treatment, what is the negative belief you have about yourself because of this event? *Circle any of the beliefs that stand out to you from the negative cognition list below.*

What do you wish you could believe about yourself instead? *Circle anything you wish to believe from the positive cognition list below.* How true does this positive belief feel to you on a scale of 1 to 7, with 1 being "completely false" and 7 being "completely true"?

Negative Cognitions	**Positive Cognitions**
I don't deserve love.	I deserve love.
I am a bad person.	I am a good/loving person.
I am terrible.	I am fine as I am.
I am worthless or inadequate.	I am worthy or worthwhile.
I am shameful.	I am honorable.
I am not good enough.	I am enough.
I deserve only bad things.	I am deserving.
I am permanently damaged.	I am okay.
I am ugly.	I am beautiful the way I am.
I should have known better.	I did the best I could at the time.
I am stupid.	I am intelligent (or able to learn).
I am insignificant or unimportant.	I am significant (or important).
I am a disappointment.	I am okay just the way I am.
I deserve to die.	I deserve to live.
I deserve to be miserable.	I deserve to be happy.
I am not in control.	I am now in control.
I am powerless or helpless.	I am capable.
I am weak.	I am strong.
I cannot get what I want.	I can get what I want.
I will fail.	I can succeed.
I have to be perfect.	I can make mistakes.
I cannot stand it.	I can handle it.
I cannot trust anyone.	I can choose whom to trust.
I cannot be trusted or cannot trust myself.	I can (learn to) trust myself.
I cannot protect myself.	I can take care of myself.
I am in danger.	It's over; I am safe now.
It's not okay to feel or show my emotions.	I can safely feel my emotions.
I cannot stand up for myself.	I can stand up for myself.
I cannot let it out.	I can choose to let it out.
I am different or don't belong.	I can be myself.

Identifying Emotions, Body Sensations, and Intensity

We are now at the final part of the protocol before we start adding bilateral stimulation. Let's identify the emotions and physical sensations you are experiencing, as well as how intense these emotions and sensations feel:

1. As you think of this issue that we are focusing on, what emotions or feelings come up for you?

2. Where do you notice these feelings and emotions in your body? Describe where in your body you notice these feelings as well as what it feels like.

3. As you notice the emotions and sensations that this issue brings up, how much does this issue or memory bother you on a scale of 0 to 10, with 0 being "not at all bothersome" and 10 being "the most something could bother you"?

> **Note:** It is important for you to stay close to the script and not go into traditional talk therapy here. You are gathering information that is going to provide you with an X-ray view of how this issue or memory is being maladaptively stored and perceived. For this reason, it is essential to stay out of the way and simply be curious about the way the client interprets the issue you are targeting by only asking the questions listed and not any others. You are not trying to understand or explore in this phase.

Identifying Emotions, Body Sensations, and Intensity

As you consider the event we are focusing on, what feelings or emotions come up for you?

Where do you notice these feelings or emotions in your body? What do these physical sensations feel like?

As you notice the emotions and sensations that this issue brings up, how distressing or bothersome does the target issue feel on a scale of 0 to 10?

0   1   2   3   4   5   6   7   8   9   10

Not at all bothersome   Extremely bothersome

Desensitization Part 1

You will now be focusing on the target issue and the details that we gathered on the last several pages as we begin to add bilateral stimulation.

You will find that as you begin this phase of EMDR, your mind will take you where you need to go. There is no right or wrong way to do EMDR, and no right or wrong thing to think about. Whatever comes up has meaning and purpose for you, even if it feels completely unrelated to the issue at hand that we start with.

One of the most inspiring and healing things about this part of EMDR is that you will discover that you have all your own answers. As your therapist, I will be here as a witness and guide during this process.

As we begin to bring up the original incident—including the worst part of the event, the negative belief that you hold because of this, and your associated emotions and body sensations—remember to just be curious. You don't have to relive this. Just let your mind go wherever it needs to go and know that there is not a right or wrong way to go about this.

Before we begin, let's take a moment to remember the resources you can use at any time during trauma processing.

Desensitization Part 1

Take a moment to remember and describe the resources you can use (if necessary) during trauma reprocessing.

Container

Restoration team

Calm, peaceful place

Anchor

Desensitization Part 2

Now that you've identified your resources, we will do 30-to-60-second sets of bilateral stimulation (or longer if needed) while you think of your target issue. During this time, it will be completely silent; you will just think on whatever comes up. After each set of bilateral stimulation, I will prompt you to pause and ask you what came up. You can share as much or as little as you desire. If you get stuck or feel blocked, let me know and I can assist you.

1. Take a deep breath in and out as we begin the bilateral stimulation. Think of the issue we are focusing on and allow your mind to notice whatever comes up.

2. Take a deep breath in and out, stop your bilateral stimulation, and tell me what you noticed or what came up for you. [*Do not talk about it—just listen and hold space.*]

3. Taking another deep breath in and out, start your bilateral stimulation and let's continue to notice that or go with that.

> **Note:** Continue with steps 2 and 3, watching for the following to occur (this will take the majority of the session):
> - **Abreaction:** The client exhibits a strong emotional response or shift.
> - **Tides are turning:** The thoughts, images, and perceptions begin to shift from more negative to more positive and hopeful.
> - **Positive shift:** New insights, realizations, or perceptions are mentioned or noticed and continue for three to five sets of BLS.

4. I would now like you to notice the original issue we started with as you think of your positive cognition. How true does that positive cognition feel to you now on a scale of 1 to 7, where 1 is "completely false" and 7 is "completely true"? [*If the positive cognition is lower than a 7, ask the client what would help them to feel this more strongly.*]

5. I would like you to notice this positive cognition, along with the issue that we started with, as we add a short set of bilateral stimulation. [*Keep the BLS to 15 seconds.*]

6. Stopping your bilateral stimulation, what did you notice? [*If they report feeling calm or relaxed, then they have successfully completed the session.*]

> **Note:** If the client becomes blocked or stuck as they work through this process, proceed to the next page: *Working Through Blocks*. If the target is not fully resolved, remind the client that processing may continue in subsequent sessions, and ask them to note anything significant that comes up for them in the meantime. You should also have the client put the issue in their container until the next session. End the session with calm place, and encourage them to reach out and use their resources if needed before you see them next.

Desensitization Part 2

Use this page to write down any stuck points, insights, or thoughts that you would like to explore further during your EMDR session.

Working Through Blocks

It is common to get stuck on certain thoughts or beliefs during EMDR. There are typically four different reasons that this can occur. I will explain some of these to you to help you better understand what may be getting in your way during reprocessing:

1. **A sense of responsibility:** You feel somewhat responsible for the event that happened to you.
2. **A lack of safety:** Your sense of safety was compromised during the event.
3. **No choice:** You felt that you didn't have a voice or a choice in the event.
4. **No control:** You felt that you had no control or were helpless during the event.

Note: When blocks occur, it is important to assist the client in working through these barriers. The following list of interweaves can be useful to jump-start blocked processing by introducing new adaptive information to the client's schema and integrating healing during desensitization.

- Can you think back to a time you remember feeling this way before?
- I am confused . . .
- I am confused—is abuse the fault of the victim?
- That's interesting . . .
- What if this were your child?
- What would you say to that part of yourself now?
- What would you say to a close friend?
- What would your restoration team tell you?
- What did that part of you need to hear or know?
- What do you wish you could have done?
- You must have a very important reason for believing that. How does that help you?
- How long should you punish yourself for this?
- Who was really responsible?
- Whose responsibility was it to keep you safe?
- Are you safe now?
- Can you choose now?
- What does this part of yourself need to heal?
- What does this part of yourself need to feel safe?
- What does this part of yourself need to forgive yourself?
- Notice how you survived.
- Who is guilty, you or them?
- Would any other person in your situation be bad too?

Working Through Blocks

Sometimes it is common to get stuck on certain thoughts or beliefs. *Place a check mark by any of the following thoughts and beliefs that you get stuck on:*

- ☐ I must have deserved this.
- ☐ I keep making the same mistakes.
- ☐ I always feel this way.
- ☐ It feels too difficult to heal.
- ☐ I don't want to think about this anymore.
- ☐ I am not sure that I will ever heal from this.
- ☐ I don't even know who I am outside of this problem.
- ☐ I say I want to solve this problem, but then I never seem to.
- ☐ It feels too difficult to get over this problem.
- ☐ Other: _____
- ☐ Other: _____
- ☐ Other: _____